The herd was furious. "Dude," said Spotz. "Keep it down. You're givin' the herd a bad rep with the chicks."

Then Bessie took a closer look.

"Hey! A cow-culator—this will help me keep track of the calves!

One plus one equals two, two plus one equals three . . ."

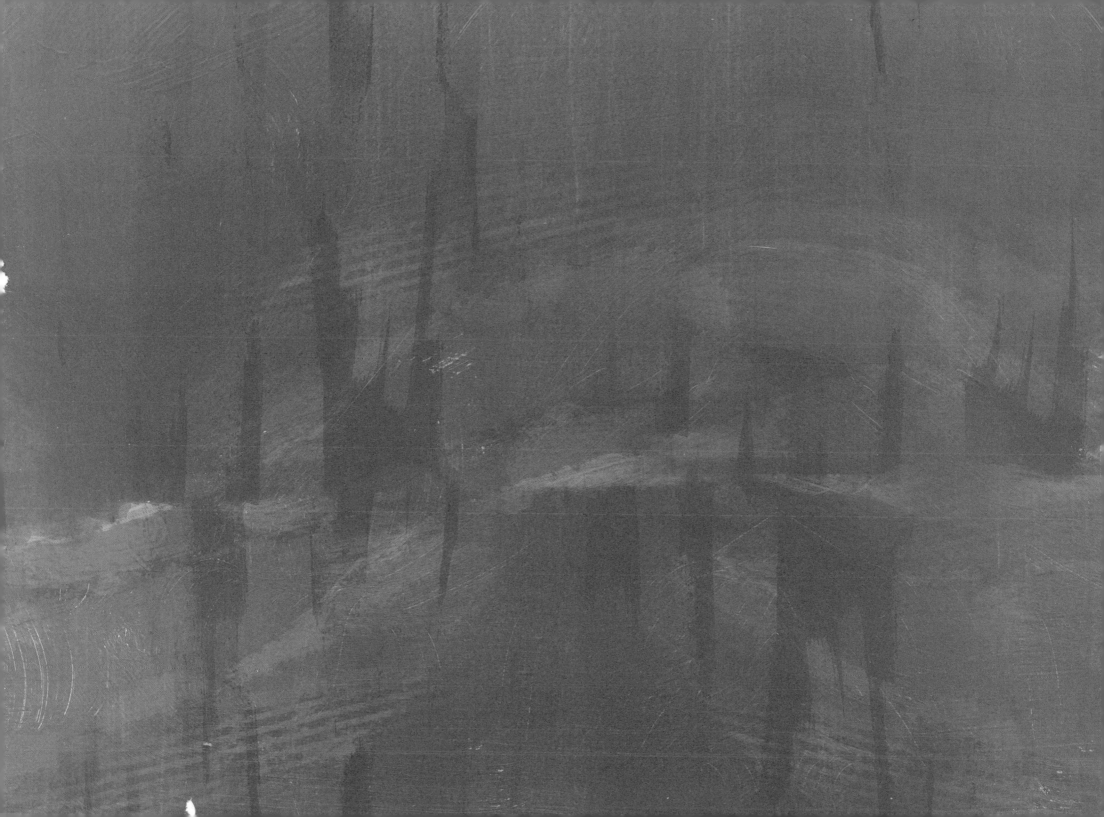

The Vietnam Experience

Tools of War

by Edgar C. Doleman, Jr.
and the editors of Boston Publishing Company

Boston Publishing Company/Boston, MA

Boston Publishing Company

President and Publisher: Robert J. George
Vice President: Richard S. Perkins, Jr.
Editor-in-Chief: Robert Manning
Managing Editor: Paul Dreyfus

Senior Writers:
Clark Dougan, Edward Doyle, David Fulghum, Samuel Lipsman, Terrence Maitland, Stephen Weiss
Senior Picture Editor: Julene Fischer

Researchers:
Jonathan Elwitt, Sandra W. Jacobs, Christy Virginia Keeny, Denis Kennedy, Michael Ludwig, Anthony Maybury-Lewis, Carole Rulnick, Nicole van Ackere, Robert Yarbrough

Picture Editors:
Wendy Johnson, Lanng Tamura
Assistant Picture Editor: Kathleen A. Reidy
Picture Researchers:
Nancy Katz Colman, Robert Ebbs, Tracey Rogers, Nana Elisabeth Stern, Shirley L. Green (Washington, D.C.), Kate Lewin (Paris)
Archivist: Kathryn J. Steeves
Picture Department Assistant:
Suzanne M. Spencer

Historical Consultants:
Vincent Demma, Lee Ewing
Technical Consultant: Steven Zaloga
Picture Consultant: Ngo Vinh Long

Staff Editor: Gordon Hardy
Production Editors:
Kerstin Gorham, Patricia Leal Welch

Editorial Production:
Sarah E. Burns, Karen E. English, Pamela George, Elizabeth Campbell Peters, Theresa M. Slomkowski, Amy P. Wilson

Design: Designworks, Sally Bindari
Design Assistants: Sherry Fatla, David Vergara

Marketing Director: Jeanne C. Gibson
Business Staff: Amy Pelletier

Special Contributors to this Volume:
John Batchelor (illustrations), Donald Dale Jackson (editorial), Anne Masters (design), Sara Schneidman (picture editor), Linda Yates (picture assistant)

About the editors and authors

Editor-in-Chief *Robert Manning*, a long-time journalist, has previously been editor-in-chief of the *Atlantic Monthly* magazine and its press. He served as assistant secretary of state for public affairs under Presidents John F. Kennedy and Lyndon B. Johnson. He has also been a fellow at the Institute of Politics at the John F. Kennedy School of Government at Harvard University.

Author: *Edgar C. Doleman, Jr.* was a company commander and intelligence officer with the 1st Cavalry Division (Airmobile) in Vietnam and later served as an infantry unit adviser with the 5th ARVN Division. He has a B.S. in physics from Virginia Military Institute and has done graduate work in history at the University of Richmond.

Historical Consultants: *Vincent H. Demma*, a historian with the U.S. Army Center of Military History, is currently working on the center's history of the Vietnam conflict. *Lee Ewing*, editor of *Army Times*, served two years in Vietnam as a combat intelligence officer with the U.S. Military Assistance Command, Vietnam (MACV) and the 101st Airborne Division.

Technical Consultant: *Steven Zaloga*, a defense writer and illustrator, is the author of numerous books on military technology.

Picture Consultant: *Ngo Vinh Long* is a social historian specializing in China and Vietnam. Born in Vietnam, he returned there most recently in 1980.

Cover Photo:

High-tech warfare. A Russian-made SA-2 surface-to-air radar-guided missile sits in a rice field near Hanoi. Although the Communists at first fought the war with defensive guerrilla tactics and rudimentary weapons, as the U.S. brought its modern arsenal to Southeast Asia the North Vietnamese and Vietcong relied increasingly on advanced weaponry supplied by their allies.

Library of Congress Catalog Card Number: 84-72888

ISBN: 0-939526-13-1

10 9 8 7 6
5 4 3 2

Contents

Preface

It is a given in war that opposing forces will bring to bear all the ingenuity and technological know-how at their command. That did not quite happen in Vietnam—the United States withheld its ultimate nuclear weapons. In most respects, though, the Vietnam War brought out all the tools of war that soldiers, scientists, and tinkerers of the 1960s and 1970s could devise. The Americans brought to bear tremendous firepower against an enemy that, early in the fighting, used some of the same primitive weapons and tactics their forebears had used long before to end 1,000 years of Chinese occupation.

But as the war—and American technology—escalated, so did the weaponry of the North Vietnamese, who acquired from their Chinese and particularly their Soviet backers air, antiaircraft, and ground weapons, many of them equal in modernity and sophistication to those employed by the Americans and South Vietnamese. It was in the end a highly technological war, but one in which will rather than technology played the decisive role.

This volume of THE VIETNAM EXPERIENCE attempts to portray for the layman some of the astonishing variety and ingenuity of the weapons and counterweapons and what it was like to use them, or face them, in Vietnam. Some were modern versions of weapons decades, even centuries, old. Some were departures for which Vietnam was merely the testing laboratory. Some were expensive, even ludicrous duds.

It would take a volume far thicker and far more technical than this one to detail them all.

—The Editors

The Technological Edge

In the beginning it looked like a modern version
of David and Goliath: the most economically productive, technologically advanced, and militarily
powerful nation on earth taking on an army of
peasant soldiers equipped with little more than
an assortment of small arms and homemade
booby traps. Indeed, when U.S. combat troops
first joined the Vietnam War in the spring of 1965,
the technological gap between the two opposing
sides was so great that the eventual outcome
seemed to many to be preordained. Through the
combined application of its vastly superior firepower, mobility, communications, and logistics,
the part of the mighty American war machine
committed to Vietnam would seek out and de-
stroy the enemy or at least wear him down to the
point where he would be forced to sue for peace.
Or so it was confidently assumed by U.S. military
leaders in Saigon and Washington.

Erroneous as that assumption proved to be, it
was based not so much upon hubris as history.

Ever since the victory of the Union over the Confederacy in the Civil War, American military planning had been shaped in large part by the nation's extraordinary productive capacity. In World War II, the U.S. "arsenal of democracy" had turned the tide, overwhelming the enemy with quantities of war materiel—aircraft and tanks, ships and artillery, rifles and uniforms—that could not be matched. When President Franklin Roosevelt called for the manufacture of 50,000 airplanes at the outset of World War II, the Germans dismissed it as a propaganda ploy. Yet by 1944 American factories were turning out nearly 100,000 planes *per year*, in addition to providing the bulk of supplies required by America's allies.

Quality over quantity

If the Second World War confirmed the advantages of unsurpassed productivity, it taught another lesson as well: that superior quality in weaponry could neutralize or overcome superior quantity. The most awesome technological development of the war, the atomic bomb, seemed to prove this with two quick strikes over Hiroshima and Nagasaki, hastening the surrender of Japan. But throughout World War II, scientists on both sides had spawned military breakthroughs with dramatic consequences for their own fight and for fights to come. Developments in radar and jet aircraft were to be the opening acts of a drama that later played itself out over Vietnam.

As the world war approached in the 1930s it was obvious that command of the sky had become critical. But air superiority could be neutralized if the defenders on the ground could track invading aircraft before they reached their targets; interceptor planes could then be sent up to engage the invaders. While American scientists invented radar, first testing it in 1932, German and British scientists were also homing in on it in the mid-1930s. By the time hostilities began in 1939 both nations had radar networks, but it was British radar that proved decisive, if only because radar was a defensive tool and in the early years of the war Britain was the defender.

English scientists proved in a secret experiment in 1935 that a plane passing through a radio field reflected radio waves back to their point of origin and thus permitted the craft's location and course to be calculated. From there, the British constructed a chain of radar stations along the coast that monitored aircraft bound for England. Each station had a 350-foot-high transmission tower with a maximum range of 120 miles. Among the several criteria for site location was a concern that the stations would not "interfere unduly with grouse shooting."

Preceding page. *America's ingenuity goes to war. Portable fuel bladders, which allow helicopters to be fueled anywhere, dot the 1st Air Cavalry's heliport at An Khe, South Vietnam, in January 1966.*

When the Germans spotted the towers in the spring of 1939 they sent a zeppelin loaded with electronic equipment on a reconnaissance cruise to find out if the British had radar, but for reasons unknown their monitoring devices failed to detect the radar signals. A few weeks later British radar picked up a squadron of more than fifty planes that approached to within seven miles of the coast and then turned back, apparently a prewar rehearsal for the bombing raids that would soon begin.

The German Luftwaffe was still unaware of the radar system the British called "Chain House" when the Battle of Britain began in the summer of 1940. A ground control network connected radar operators with British Royal Air Force pilots long before Nazi planes reached England. Also assisting British air defenses was "Ultra," or the "Turing engine," named for its developer, cryptanalyst Alan Turing. Kept secret until the end of the war, Ultra was an ingenious device used to break the Germans' highly complex system of codes. With the information provided by radar and the decoding of German messages, the pilots could concentrate their outnumbered forces—the Germans had a five-to-one edge at the beginning—where it would pay off. "I was astonished," a German airman admitted later, "to find that each time we crossed the Channel there was always an enemy fighter force in position." Along with the Ultra decoder, radar was the equalizer that resulted in the destruction of 1,736 German planes as against RAF losses of 915. Technology in this instance had saved a nation from disaster.

Three years later it was British pilots who were trying to dodge German radar over the Fatherland, and this time ingenuity served aggression. British experts discovered that strips of aluminum foil precisely thirty centimeters long interfered with German radar. Bundles of foil tossed from British planes filled German radar screens with a blizzard of signals that made the receivers useless, a technique at the time given the code name "Window" and later called "chaff." With German fighters thus forced to scramble blindly, a fleet of 722 British bombers slammed Hamburg in July 1943 with one of the most devastating aerial barrages ever unleashed. Nine square miles of the city were consumed in the first-ever firestorm that resulted in 50,000 people dead and 1 million homeless.

At about the same time, Germans and Americans were involved in a high-technology duel over the skies of Italy. In 1943, the Germans began deploying a number of types of radio-guided glide bombs and missiles, launched from aircraft, against Allied shipping in the Mediterranean. These were the first true precision guided munitions and the precursors to the "smart bombs" first used by the U.S. in Vietnam. In August 1943, the British sloop HMS *Egret* was sunk by an Hs–293 missile, and subsequently this type of missile knocked out one Greek and four British destroyers. The German Fritz X glide bomb also damaged or destroyed a number of warships. In response to this aerial threat, the Naval Research Lab developed the first radio jamming system and used it to interfere with the channels over which the German weapons were guided. This was deployed aboard American destroyers in October 1943, and was very successful in cutting down the effectiveness of the German missiles.

Almost a year to the day after the bombardment of Hamburg, RAF pilot Alan Wall was approaching Munich in his Mosquito photo reconnaissance plane when he spotted a craft unlike anything he had ever seen closing on his tail at blazing speed. Wall tried to outmaneuver his attacker, but the German pilot overtook him repeatedly and blasted away with 30MM cannons, scoring several hits before Wall found sanctuary in a cloud bank and escaped to Italy. The streamlined, swift plane Wall encountered that morning in July 1944 was the Messerschmitt 262, the world's first operational jet fighter. With a top speed of 540 miles per hour, it was 70 mph faster than any of the Allies' propeller-driven craft. The Me-262 was quite simply the best airplane in existence and a weapon that could well have affected the outcome of the war.

Jet propulsion, like radar, was a notion that scientists in several countries pursued in the decade before the war. But German researchers, aided by early government backing, were first to prove that a plane could be propelled by the thrust from a turbojet engine, first to test fly a jet plane (in 1939), and first to embark on production (1944). Though Britain, the U.S., and Japan all developed jets before the war ended, the Germans were the leaders.

Allied commanders quickly saw the danger that the Me-262 represented. Squadrons of German jets attacked Allied installations and armored columns on the western front from just above treetop level. The speed of another German jet, the Ar-234, enabled it to fly photo reconnaissance missions with little fear of interference, and the resultant intelligence contributed to the success of the German counteroffensive in the Ardennes in late 1944. American and British fighters had to scramble to keep the jets in sight; hitting them was almost impossible.

The Germans cleverly dispersed and camouflaged manufacturing sites and jet bases to make them more difficult to spot, but by April 1945 Allied bomber crews were regularly lambasting the jet bases and soon afterward Me-262 squadrons had to scatter to far-off fields. It was none too soon. As Allied troops advanced into Germany they repeatedly came upon rows of newly built jet fighters awaiting delivery to now-defunct Luftwaffe squadrons. The main reason the Messerschmitts had not been used widely was that U.S. bombers had wiped out their fuel. The jet was also very difficult to pilot.

In the final weeks of the war, both U.S. and Soviet forces seized several Me-262s along with their factories and technical files. Designers in both countries saw that the jet's powerful engines made its extraordinary speed possible. Combining this with still-experimental swept-

Top. *A British worker examines a pile of radar-foiling aluminum strips early in World War II.* Below. *The "chaff" is tossed from a British Lancaster bomber during a raid on Essen, Germany, in March 1945.*

back wings and some of their own ideas, Russian engineers came up with the MiG-15, which made its public debut in 1948. In the U.S. the North American Aviation Company incorporated the swept wing design into its F-86 Sabrejet, which at 675 miles per hour became the speediest operational American fighter, although it was slower than the MiG. A few years later these two stepchildren of the Me-262 tangled in the sky over North

Technology in the Great War

The trenches of World War I created battlefields bloodier than perhaps any others in history. As the "Great War" began, commanders of both forces hoped tactical measures including surprise, maneuver, or overwhelming mass could generate sufficient momentum in an initial assault to overcome the entrenched enemy. But nothing seemed to break the muddy embrace of trench warfare. The Germans tried to advance at Verdun in 1916, but ten months of battle later nothing had changed except that 698,000 men had been killed or wounded in an area the size of Manhattan. In all of 1915, the Allies never gained more than three miles of territory.

The technology of the time played a large part in commanders' hopes, but a host of new weapons was brought to the front to little avail. The tank, introduced by the British, made its first appearance but was so unreliable that it had little effect on any battle. At Cambrai in 1917, for example, tanks broke through the German line but mechanical failure and lack of reserves prevented them from sustaining the attack.

Of all the major forces the Americans came the least technologically prepared. When they joined the war in 1917, they had no tanks or artillery and had to use French machine guns and aircraft. Still, in the ultimate war of attrition, the Americans, with their fresh courage and sheer numbers, proved the final straw for an exhausted Germany.

A British Mark I "male" tank advances in the Somme on September 15, 1916. Inset. At Bellicourt in 1918, Mark IV tanks advance carrying metal fascines to drop across trenches. World War I tanks had an average speed of two mph and a range of fifteen to twenty miles.